The True Princess

Angela Elwell Hunt
Illustrated by Diana Magnuson

Charisma
KIDS
A STRANG COMPANY

The True Princess
ISBN 1-59185-633-7
Copyright © 2004 by Angela Elwell Hunt
Requests for information may be addressed to:

A STRANG COMPANY

The children's book imprint of Strang Communications Company
600 Rinehart Rd., Lake Mary, FL 32746
www.charismakids.com

Children's Editor: Pat Matuszak
Illustrations by Diana Magnuson
Designed by Michael Boze

Library of Congress Catalog Card Number: 2004108003

This book was previously published by Chariot Books, an imprint of David C. Cook
Publishing Co., ISBN 1-55513-760-1, copyright © 1992.

Printed in the United States of America
05 06 07 08 — 5 4 3 2

For Taryn, my little princess

Once upon a time, in a faraway land, there lived a generous king who had one lovely little daughter. She was always beautifully dressed in silk dresses and jewels. Poets wrote poems to praise her sweet smile and musicians sang songs about her beautiful golden hair.

Whatever she needed was provided. Whatever she wanted was given to her. There were maids to dress her, singers to sing for her, and jokers to make her laugh. But best of all, there was Nana, who took care of her, and her father the king, who loved her.

One day, however, the king heard news of trouble in another kingdom. "I must go away on a long journey to help a friend," he told his daughter. "You must remain here with Nana."

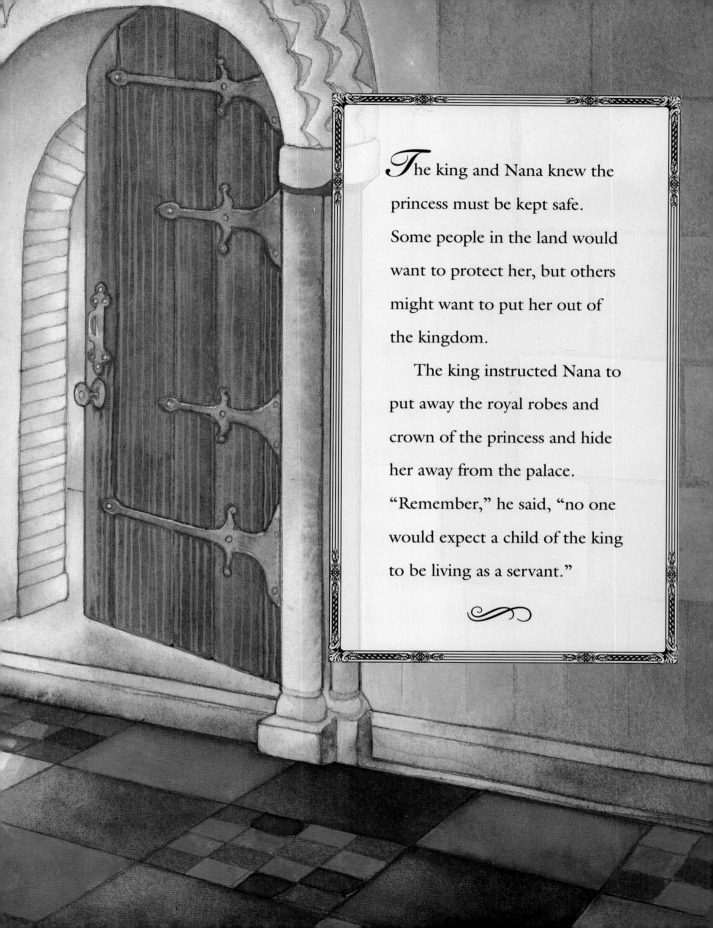

The king and Nana knew the princess must be kept safe. Some people in the land would want to protect her, but others might want to put her out of the kingdom.

The king instructed Nana to put away the royal robes and crown of the princess and hide her away from the palace. "Remember," he said, "no one would expect a child of the king to be living as a servant."

When the time came to say good-bye, the princess was worried. "Father," she asked, "how can I live outside the palace? Who will feed me? Who will dress me? Who will sing for me? Who will make me laugh?"

The king smiled. "One day you will help me rule this kingdom," he told her, "but now you have much to learn."

He placed his gentle hand on her head. "Nana will be with you," he promised. "She is following my wishes so you will never be out of my care."

The people of the kingdom searched everywhere, but no one could find a beautiful princess with long golden hair and lovely royal robes.

While the people searched, Nana and the princess settled in the center of town over a little bakery shop where they worked together. "If we want to eat, we must bake," Nana said simply. "We will bake cakes, pies, and breads to eat and sell."

On their first morning in the
little bakery house, the princess
woke and murmured, "Dress
me, please, Nana."

"My dear girl, I simply
don't have time," replied Nana,
slipping into her baking dress
and apron. "But if you will be
kind enough to tie my apron, I
promise I'll tie yours."

So the princess learned to
dress herself.

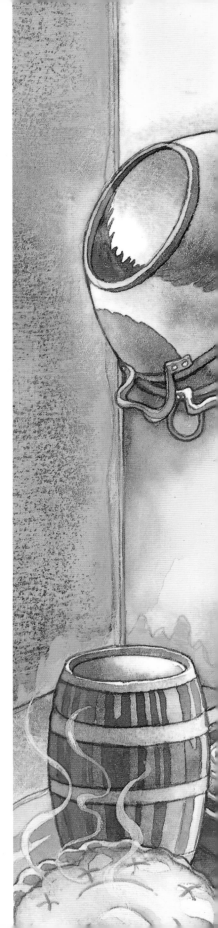

After several weeks of baking, the princess was exhausted. "Nana, there is no time to listen to music," she complained. "Why can't we stop working and call in the singers?"

"My dear girl," said Nana, "songs from your own heart would be more refreshing."

So the princess learned to sing while she worked.

$\mathcal{A}$nother day the princess put too much yeast in a loaf of bread and the dough exploded —POP—all over the room. She looked at the mess and sighed. She called to Nana in the next room: "Nana, can't we call in the jokers? I need to laugh again."

When Nana looked in and saw the mess, she burst into a fit of giggles. "Who needs jokers?" she said. "Take a look in the mirror."

The princess did—and she learned to laugh at herself.

$\mathcal{N}$ow when the princess could not be found, many girls in the kingdom thought they could take her place when the king returned. They spent hours designing and sewing lovely royal robes and grew their hair long and stood in the sun for hours so that it reflected the sun's golden rays.

They made fun of the girl from the bakery because she was too busy working to try to look like them. "Poor little muffin-maker," they called as she ran by making deliveries. "You don't have what it takes to be a princess."

But the bakery girl just laughed and hummed a little song to herself as she hurried by.

*A*fter many, many months the king returned. His guards and servants escorted him immediately to his palace and announced that the king would receive his daughter the next morning.

$\mathcal{T}$he next morning when the palace guards

announced, "The princess is here!", the king was

surprised to see twenty-five young ladies waiting for

him. They all had long golden hair and were wearing

royal robes. A twenty-sixth girl stood quietly in a

patched dress at the back of the room.

The king smiled at the crowd of beauties. "So many princesses?" he asked. He paused in front of the first girl. "Would you mind helping my servant put on his cloak?"

The girl frowned. "A true princess," she sniffed, "does not dress *anyone*. She has maids to do that."

$\mathcal{T}$he king stopped in front of the second girl.
"Would you mind singing a song or two for the
kitchen helpers? They would enjoy it so much."

The second girl smiled a little smile. "Princesses
do not sing for cooks," she murmured. "They hire
singers to sing for *them*."

The king paused in front of a third girl. "Would you tell my soldiers a funny story?" he asked. "They are tired from our long trip."

"Call the royal jokers," she suggested. "That is what a *real* princess would do."

The king looked at the young ladies before him. "Is there anyone here who would sing for me? Tell a joke? Serve me in any way?"

The quiet girl in the patched dress spoke up. "I'd be happy to, Sire," she whispered. "Because I love you."

"My darling child," said the king, hugging his daughter close. "It is love that marks a true daughter of the king."

So the king and his princess were reunited, and it has been said that no princess ever was kinder, more loving, or a wiser ruler than she was.

And no one in the world could bake a better pie.

Think About It

"... Whoever wants to become great
among you must be your servant, and
whoever wants to be first must be your
slave—just as the Son of Man did not
come to be served, but to serve, and to
give his life as a ransom for many."
—*Matthew 20:26–28*